Astronauts and Cosmonauts

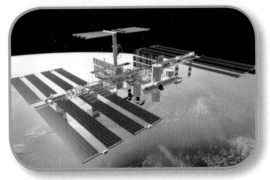

by Joanna Korba

PEARSON

Scott Foresman

Editorial Offices: Glenview, Illinois • Parsippany, New Jersey • New York, New York
Sales Offices: Needham, Massachusetts • Duluth, Georgia • Glenview, Illinois
Coppell, Texas • Ontario, California • Mesa, Arizona

Opener ©Bettmann/Corbis; 1 ©Royalty-Free/Corbis; 3 ©Tony Freeman/PhotoEdit; 4 ©Marc Garanger/Corbis, 4 ©Bettmann/Corbis; 7 ©Kazak Sergei/ITAR-TASS/Corbis; 9 ©Jim Sugar/Corbis; 10 ©Rykoff Collection/Corbis; 12 ©Rykoff Collection/Corbis; 13 NASA; 15 ©Bettmann/Corbis; 16 ©NASA/Roger Ressmeyer/Corbis; 19 Carol Stutz; 20 ©Royalty-Free/Corbis

ISBN: 0-328-13570-4

From the dawn of human history, people have gazed at the heavens in wonder. Early cultures created myths to explain why the night sky was sprinkled with stars. Over the centuries, earthbound observers and scientists gathered knowledge about the heavens. They learned that, out there in the vastness of space, other planets existed beyond ours.

In 1955, two countries boldly declared that they planned to take a closer look at these other worlds. Both the United States and the Soviet Union—which was a nation made up of Russia and its neighbors—announced their intention to launch artificial satellites. This was no joint mission, however. The two countries were fierce rivals.

The Race

This rivalry between nations grew after World War II, and the quest for space-age technology grew out of both nations' desire to have the most accurate, most powerful defense systems. At first the United States put more research into bombers, while the Soviet Union focused their research on missiles. That is how the Soviet Union made unexpected advances in rocket technology.

While the United States was still deep in the development of its first satellite, the Soviet Union astonished the world by launching its satellite, *Sputnik*, on October 4, 1957. *Sputnik* means "traveling companion" in Russian. About the size of a basketball and weighing 183 pounds, tiny *Sputnik* managed to orbit Earth in just 98 minutes. One

In 1957, the Soviet Union sent *Sputnik* and *Sputnik II* into space.

4

month later, the Soviets sent up *Sputnik II* with a dog named Laika inside.

The United States, caught off guard when the Soviet Union had beaten them into space, vowed to catch up to their rivals—and pull ahead. The "space race" had begun.

The first satellites launched by the United States— *Explorer 1* and *Vanguard 1*—were significantly smaller than either *Sputnik* or *Sputnik II*. U.S. rockets at the time were much less powerful than their Soviet counterparts.

As part of its commitment to the space race, the United States created the National Aeronautics and Space Administration, known more commonly as NASA. This civilian agency centralized the efforts of politicians, the military, the **aerospace** industry, and university researchers.

One of NASA's publicly stated goals was to launch a person into space. The Soviets were not so open about their objectives. They worked hard to keep their missions and timetables secret from the rest of the world—and especially from the United States. But everyone knew that it was only a matter of time before human beings—Americans or Soviets—would be sent into space.

Interestingly, the two countries used remarkably similar terms for their would-be space travelers. Both drew on the Greek word for sailor, *nautes*. The Soviets combined *nautes* with the Greek word *cosmos*, meaning "universe." They called their space travelers *cosmonauts*. The United States combined *nautes* with the Greek word *astron*, meaning "star," to come up with the term *astronauts*.

The Training

As their space programs went forward, the United States and the Soviet Union developed intensive training programs for the human beings they planned to send into space. There were—and still are—similarities and differences in the training of astronauts and cosmonauts.

Both astronauts and cosmonauts were expected to be extremely fit, undergoing **strenuous** exercise programs and maintaining healthful diets. Astronaut and cosmonaut physical training was similar, although the Soviet model tended to be more structured and strictly planned.

Astronauts were primarily educated in "hands-on" situations. NASA relied heavily on training **simulators**, or "sims." These mechanical devices attempted to imitate the flight conditions that astronauts would be likely to encounter in space.

The first United States astronauts were selected from among military test pilots and engineers for what was named the Mercury Program. Since no one really knew what situations actually awaited a human venturing outside Earth's atmosphere, many of the simulations that NASA developed were a matter of educated guesswork. The Mercury astronauts worked with NASA engineers to build simulations. In that way, the astronauts helped train the people who were finding ways to train the astronauts!

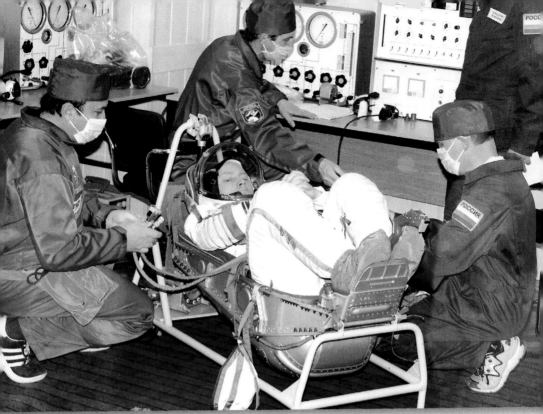

Astronauts and cosmonauts must pass a battery of physical tests before being cleared for a space mission.

By contrast, the Soviets relied more on pencil-and-paper training. Cosmonauts were mainly taught in a classroom setting, rather than in simulators. They listened to instructors, took notes, asked questions, and then took oral examinations on what they had learned.

Cosmonaut training continues to be largely in the classroom, although simulators are now used as well. Recently, NASA added formal testing to its astronaut training, although it still relies heavily on "sims."

While their training may have differed in some ways, it was directed to the same challenge. Both astronauts and cosmonauts had to learn how to live and work under conditions found nowhere on Earth. For example, they had to become accustomed to weightlessness.

Every bit of matter, whether it is large or small, pulls on every other bit of matter. This is what is called gravitational force. Earth exerts this force on every object found on its surface, including us. We refer to Earth's gravitational force as **gravity**. One of the major challenges facing space travelers is that gravitational force is either very weak—almost entirely lacking—in outer space. Everything not tied down—objects, living things, even liquids—simply floats about in a spaceship, basically weightlessly.

How could the United States' and Soviet training programs simulate weightlessness? They came up with similar solutions. The Soviets mounted a simulated spacecraft cabin in a Tupolev-104, a twin-engine passenger jet plane. The cosmonauts entered this cabin. Then the plane soared straight up, turned quickly, and dived downward. Everything on board, including the cosmonauts, became weightless for about half a minute.

The astronauts, meanwhile, were training on a special KC-135 plane affectionately known as the "vomit comet." This plane was flown in a similar manner to the Soviet's Tupolev-104 and produced the same thirty seconds of weightlessness.

Some trainees get sick during their half-minute of weightlessness. Those that do are likely to suffer initially from spacesickness when in space.

Another kind of "weightlessness" training is used for astronauts who are going to be wearing bulky spacesuits as they walk—and work—in space. Much of the training is done in a specialized swimming pool. Although not weightless, the astronaut maneuvering around in water in a spacesuit gets a feel for what it will be like floating in space.

Today's astronauts train underwater in huge tanks fitted out as space shuttle chambers and as the International Space Station. With such training, astronauts will be familiar with conditions on these craft before they actually board them.

The First People in Space

After the surprise of the *Sputnik* launch, the United States vowed to catch up with the Soviets and surpass them. In 1961, NASA announced that it would be sending the first human being into space. The launch was set for May 5, and the astronaut selected was Mercury astronaut Alan B. Shepard, Jr. The Soviets, working in secret, redoubled their efforts to be the first nation to launch a human into space. They succeeded—by barely three weeks.

On April 12, 1961, a Soviet Air Force pilot named Yuri A. Gagarin became the first human to travel into space. His spaceship was named *Vostok 1*. *Vostok* means "east." *Vostok 1* was controlled by an automatic guidance system. In other words, Yuri Gagarin was not flying the spacecraft himself. *Vostok 1* took 108 minutes to orbit Earth once before landing safely.

After his historic flight, Gagarin did not fly again but continued to work on the Soviet space program. The banner here says, "12 April 1961, *Vostok*."

The United States continued with its scheduled launch. Shepard flew inside a cone-shaped capsule named *Freedom 7* that weighed about 3,000 pounds. The capsule was launched into space at the tip of a tall rocket. As the rocket sped out of Earth's atmosphere, parts of it fell away as they were no longer needed.

Shepard lay on a contour couch during his brief fifteen-minute flight. Shepard had hoped to orbit Earth, as Gagarin did, but NASA decided just to send him into space and have him quickly return back to Earth.

The first American to orbit Earth was John H. Glenn, Jr., in the *Friendship 7*. On February 20, 1962, he completed three orbits around Earth in less than five hours. During that short time, he maneuvered the capsule into different positions, tested its various positions, and observed some dramatic events, which he described for those back on Earth—including a giant dust storm in Africa, a sunrise, and a sunset!

On June 16, 1963, the Soviets scored another first. Cosmonaut Valentina Tereshkova, a Soviet pilot, made forty-five orbits aboard *Vostok 6* in a flight that lasted just under seventy-one hours. She was the first woman to travel into outer space.

Alexei Leonov was the first man to walk in space.

The First Space Walk

The first human "walked" in space on March 18, 1965, when cosmonaut Alexei Leonov, who had trained for two years, calmly stepped out into the void of outer space. A camera mounted on the outside of the capsule enabled millions of Soviet TV viewers to share the moment with him.

There was a tense moment, though, when Leonov tried to reenter his spacecraft. During the space walk, his spacesuit had expanded a bit. He had to slowly and carefully let air out of the suit before he was able to fit through the hatch and enter the capsule once again.

Less than three months later, on June 3, Ed White became the first American to walk in space. His two-man flight (he was accompanied by James A. McDivitt) lasted four days, but his space walk lasted only twenty-one minutes.

During the first minutes of the walk, White used a handheld oxygen-jet gun to propel himself away from the capsule and to the end of his lifeline. He did this several times. When the fuel in the gun ran out, White had to twist and turn and maneuver his tether to get back to the hatch!

The First Moon Walk

The Soviets had accomplished a number of historic firsts in the space race. But the grand prize was looming on the horizon, and it would go to the first nation to land a human on Earth's moon.

The grand prize went to the United States. People all over the world were glued to their television sets on July 20, 1969, as the lunar module *Eagle* touched down on our nearest neighbor in space. Six hours later, the doors of the *Eagle* opened. Astronaut Neil A. Armstrong emerged in his bulky spacesuit, climbed down the ladder of the *Eagle,* and uttered his now famous words as he stepped onto the moon: "That's one small step for man; one giant leap for mankind."

He was soon joined on the moon by his *Eagle* crewmate Buzz Aldrin. The two astronauts spent about two-and-a-half hours gathering moon rocks, taking photographs, and drilling core samples from the moon's surface. They planted the American flag at their landing site and left a plaque behind. It said, "We came in peace for all mankind."

Teamwork in Space

Since the space race began, the United States and the Soviet Union had been locked in fierce competition. That situation began to change in the early 1970s. In 1972, the two former rivals agreed to work together on what came to be called the *Apollo-Soyuz* Test Project. It was the first human spacecraft mission to be coordinated by two nations. The goal of the project was for a U.S. *Apollo* spacecraft and a Soviet *Soyuz* spacecraft to **rendezvous** in space, maneuver into position, and attempt to dock.

The American *Apollo* spacecraft was the same design as those used on flights to the moon. The *Soyuz* (meaning "union") had been the Soviets' primary spacecraft since 1967. Each nation's spacecraft had been developed independently. The test project would enable the two countries to check the compatibility of their systems in hopes of paving the way for future joint space projects.

The plan called for the *Soyuz* to go up first, with the *Apollo* arriving later for the rendezvous. For practical reasons, and also as a sign of cooperation and respect, the Americans agreed to speak Russian for the mission, while the Soviets agreed to speak English. Everyone involved on the project had to learn the design and systems of the other country's spacecraft.

The mission began on July 15, 1975, with the launch of *Soyuz*. *Apollo* left seven hours later. The successful docking took place on the afternoon of July 21. Then two astronauts entered *Soyuz*, exchanged gifts with the cosmonauts, and shared a meal together. The next day, two cosmonauts entered *Apollo*.

After the two spacecrafts separated, they remained in space for a few days before returning to Earth. The mission was judged to be an enormous success. It proved that crewmembers could transfer from one spacecraft to another. It enabled crewmembers to conduct a number of important scientific experiments. The United States and the Soviet Union were able to work together effectively, rather than compete against each other. It was a huge leap forward for international cooperation.

The commander of the *Soyuz* was Alexei Leonov, the first human to walk in space. The *Apollo* was under the command of Thomas P. Stafford.

The Mir Space Station

On February 20, 1986, the Soviets launched a space station that they called *Mir* (meaning "peace"). *Mir* contained two docking ports, one at either end, and four hatches. The hatches were designed to accommodate the attachment of laboratory modules. When the station was fully operational, *Mir* would form the hub of a rimless wheel that had four laboratory "spokes" radiating from it.

Completing the space station would take time. Only so much equipment and supplies could be brought up at a time. As the station was gradually being assembled, a crew of cosmonauts was constantly on board, except for a few months in 1989. Each crew might spend several months in space before replacements arrived.

After the Soviet Union dissolved in 1991, Russia (which had been the largest Soviet republic) took over *Mir*. In 1992, Russia entered into a joint project with the United States known as *Shuttle-Mir*. The plan was for astronauts and cosmonauts to work together as a team on board the *Mir*. Each shuttle mission would bring up needed supplies, as well as a fresh crew to relieve the team members who had been in space for some time. Eventually, other countries became involved as well.

After some preliminary attempts, the first successful shuttle docking took place on *Mir* in late June 1994. The shuttle *Atlantis*, with two cosmonauts aboard, replaced the crew (two cosmonauts and an astronaut) that had come up a few months earlier on a Russian *Soyuz* capsule.

On *Mir*, scientists who were part of the cosmonaut/astronaut teams performed a number of valuable experiments. For example, seeds were planted to see how they would **germinate** and develop in space. Also, protein crystals were produced that are now being used in medical and scientific research.

Although the *Mir* maintained a steady, breathable mixture of air, it could not maintain a strong enough gravitational force to keep crewmembers from floating.

Mir's crews gathered important data regarding human beings' ability to live in space over time. The crewmembers, after all, were living in space for several months. There was much less gravity on *Mir* than on Earth. Researchers discovered that a person's bones could get weak quite quickly in space. The weakening was most pronounced on the hips and the spine. To combat this condition, the astronauts and cosmonauts on board had to do special exercises to help them maintain their bones and muscles.

In June 1997, an accident crippled *Mir*. A cosmonaut was trying to dock an unmanned spacecraft to the laboratory module (called Spektr). The craft collided with Spektr, opening up a small hole. When Spektr began to leak air, the crew had to disable its power cables and close the hatch that connected it to *Mir*. Although the crew lost some valuable scientific data, a remarkable salvage effort saved much of the work.

Soon after the accident, a mission arrived with replacements for the **beleaguered** crew. During this time, cosmonaut Vladimir Titov, in a U.S. spacesuit, ventured out on a space walk with astronaut Scott Parazynski. It was the first time a cosmonaut had been dressed as an astronaut!

After the damage to *Mir* was repaired, work on the space station continued until 2001. In March of 2001, Russia guided *Mir* back to Earth, knowing it would be destroyed during reentry. Most of it burned up as it entered Earth's atmosphere, and the rest fell harmlessly into the Pacific Ocean.

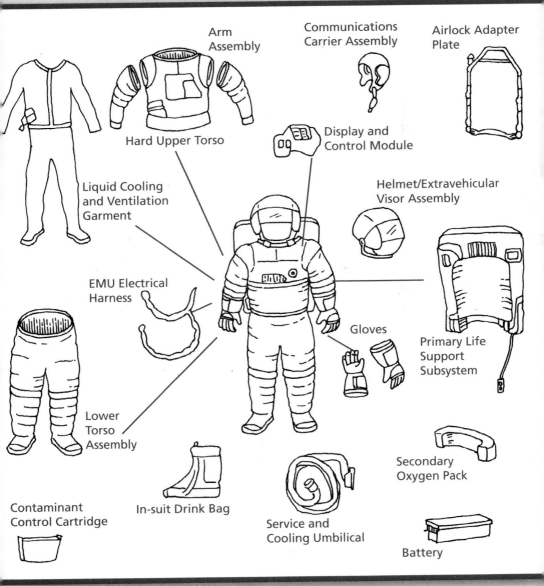

Arm Assembly

Communications Carrier Assembly

Airlock Adapter Plate

Hard Upper Torso

Display and Control Module

Liquid Cooling and Ventilation Garment

Helmet/Extravehicular Visor Assembly

EMU Electrical Harness

Gloves

Primary Life Support Subsystem

Lower Torso Assembly

Secondary Oxygen Pack

Contaminant Control Cartridge

In-suit Drink Bag

Service and Cooling Umbilical

Battery

The International Space Station

In 1984, then President Ronald Reagan authorized NASA to design a large, permanent space station. Eventually, the United States collaborated with Russia, Brazil, Canada, Japan, and the European Space Agency to create the station's final design and build it. Work began in 1998 and continued for many years afterward.

In 2000, the first crew came aboard—two cosmonauts and an astronaut—and proceeded to move into the station. The people who would later come to work here were from a number of different countries. It is an international space station, after all. In many ways, these people carry on the work that was done on *Mir*—maintaining a station in space and conducting scientific experiments. And as they

do their jobs, they (and scientists back on Earth) learn how to make living and working in space better and safer. There is still much to learn. For example, how long can people survive safely in reduced gravity? Will human beings ever be able to build homes in outer space?

We have come a long way from the days of the space race, when American astronauts and Russian cosmonauts were bitter rivals. Not only have our two countries found ways to work together, but other countries have joined in as well. People of all nations have come together to learn and experiment as we humans look for ways to live among the stars.

Now Try This

Make a Plan for a Space Vacation

Everybody's talking about taking this year's vacation in space. Suppose you had to plan a space vacation. Just follow the instructions on the next page. Here is a poem to inspire your ideas.

Come swim in the air,
in the air so fair
with no gravity.
Come live and dine,
on a diet so fine,
there'll be no cavities.

Be gardeners, plant seeds
for protein needs.
Come stay in the space station.
Work out and get strong,
you can sing all day long
on your space vacation.

Come for a vacation in space.
It is just the right place
to relax at your own pace.
And just in case
you need a race—
then race to our vacation in space.

1. Design a vacation hotel for space. Begin by making a list of ways that this hotel will be different from one on Earth. Consider the problem of no gravity.
2. Think about the types of things people might want to do when they are on vacation in space. How can your hotel help them do these things? Write a paragraph to describe your answers.
3. How will people get to your hotel from Earth? Write a brief paragraph explaining the travel route.
4. Make a diagram of your hotel. Label different areas of the hotel.
5. Create a brochure for your hotel. Remember that the brochure should make people want to visit your hotel.

Glossary

aerospace *adj.* related to the science and technology of flight.

beleaguered *adj.* beset by troubles.

germinate *v.* to begin to sprout or grow, as a plant from a seed.

gravity *n.* the force of gravitation on Earth, pulling everything toward its center.

rendezvous *v.* to meet at a particular time and place.

simulator *n.* an apparatus or a device that creates test conditions that are as close as possible to real-life conditions.

strenuous *adj.* requiring much energy and effort.